Divine
Cupcakes

First published in 2009 by New Holland Publishers (NZ) Ltd
Auckland • Sydney • London • Cape Town

www.newhollandpublishers.co.nz

218 Lake Road, Northcote, Auckland 0627, New Zealand
Unit 1, 66 Gibbes Street, Chatswood, NSW 2067, Australia
86–88 Edgware Road, London W2 2EA, United Kingdom
80 McKenzie Street, Cape Town 8001, South Africa

Commissioned and project managed by Louise Armstrong
Edited by Fiona McRae
Designed by Rachel Kirkland at The Fount

National Library of New Zealand Cataloguing-in-Publication Data

Jane, Tamara.
Divine cupcakes : a book of temptation / written by Tamara
Jane ; photography by Adam Toomer and Danielle Saudino.
Includes index.
ISBN 978-1-86966-250-9
1. Cupcakes. I. Toomer, Adam. II. Saudino, Danielle. III. Title.
641.8653—dc 22

10 9 8 7 6 5 4

Colour reproduction by Pica Digital Pte Ltd, Singapore
Printed in China by Toppan Leefung Printing Ltd, on paper sourced from
sustainable forests.

Cadbury and Crunchie are registered trade marks of Cadbury Group and
are used with their permission.
Sanitarium and Weet-Bix are registered trade marks of Sanitarium and
are used with their permission.

Divine
Cupcakes

A book of temptation

TAMARA JANE

Photography by Danielle Saudino & Adam Toomer

NEW HOLLAND

Contents

Cupcake recipes

Celebration cakes

Toppings & frostings

88

Decorations

98

Foreword

Food may be a staple of our daily existence, but it is the artisans of the world who inspire us to be passionate about food. Tamara Jane is such an artisan and this book is an expression of that passion: revealed in her recipes, in her detailed approach and – along with photographers Danielle Saudino and Adam Toomer – in the love and care that has been invested in every single page of this book.

If you have a sweet tooth, I have no doubt you will enjoy tempting your friends and family with Tamara's irresistible cupcakes. Enjoy!

Bruce Robertson
Chief Executive
Hospitality Association of New Zealand

Introduction

Cupcakes are an irresistible temptation – and rightly so. There is nothing on earth quite like the sheer bliss we experience as we take that first bite of a sinfully rich cupcake – knowing full well there is no way we are going to share.

I love making cupcakes. I love the way people smile when they first set eyes on the small, beautifully decorated creations I've made and the delight they take in selecting one for someone special or to treat themselves. Take the time to learn the art of cupcake-making and you will be sure to win the hearts of those around you.

Accurately measuring the ingredients is vital to your cupcake success. I use electronic scales to weigh dry ingredients as this ensures ingredients are not packed too tightly into measuring cups, or not firmly enough. If you are using cup measures, be sure to use metric cups.

Oven temperature is also paramount for ensuring you end up with well-risen and perfectly baked cakes. Fan-baking dries out small cakes quickly so, if you are using a fan oven, reduce the temperature stated in each recipe by 10 degrees and watch the cooking time.

Most importantly, have fun decorating your cupcakes. Play around with colours and flavours and develop something unique for your family or friends. Make it a day with the kids: let everyone have a go making funky flowers or imaginative animals out of modelling paste. Remember, bowls of simple sprinkles, chocolate buttons and assorted sweets can have just as much impact as more sophisticated decorations. Cupcake decorating is all about personal taste, imagination and suitability for an occasion.

There are some basic rules when making cupcakes: if you follow them, you should have no difficulty producing excellent cupcakes. On page 17 you will find my golden rules for ensuring you produce perfect cupcakes every time.

Good luck and enjoy!

The right ingredients

Most cupcake ingredients should be available from your supermarket. However, you may need to purchase some items from a specialty cake-decoration supplier, such as paste food colouring, glitter and fondant icing.

Butter

I use unsalted butter as salted butter can alter the taste of a cake. It is easier to add a small amount of salt if required. In those cases where added salt is required it is included in the ingredients list of the recipe.

Have butter at room temperature when you begin. If the butter is too cold it may be microwaved on low power until just soft, but make sure you don't melt it.

Chocolate

Always use the best quality you can afford. As a guide, the higher the cocoa-butter content the richer and smoother the taste. Compound chocolate sold as melts or cooking chocolate does not give an intense flavour to cakes.

To melt chocolate successfully, place chopped pieces in a heatproof bowl over a saucepan of gently simmering water and stir until smooth and glossy. Make sure the chocolate does not come into contact with the water – if it does the chocolate will seize and stiffen.

Alternatively, chocolate can be melted in a microwave on medium power. Stir the chocolate after one minute, repeat in 15 second bursts, stirring after each burst, until the chocolate is completely melted.

Eggs

All the recipes in this book use large eggs (approximately 65g or size seven).

Eggs need to be at room temperature to allow for easy blending into the mixture. To bring eggs to room temperature you can place them in a basin of warm water for 10 minutes.

Milk

Always use full-fat milk. Low-fat milk will inevitably produce cakes with an inferior taste and consistency. Ensure milk is at room temperature before adding to cake batter otherwise the mixture will thicken, resulting in tough cakes.

Refrigerated milk may be warmed in a small jug in the microwave to bring it to room temperature before adding to cake batter.

Raising agents

Baking soda and baking powder are not interchangeable ingredients and must be used in the precise amount specified. Too little or too much will cause dramatically different results.

I often use plain flour and baking powder instead of self-raising flour as this gives more control over the amount of rise in the final product.

Sugar

When a recipe calls for caster sugar, use a well-known brand as the grains will be finer and dissolve more quickly into the mixture. Standard white sugar is too coarse and will change the final product.

Muscovado, brown or dark-brown sugar are all interchangeable with only a slight change in the flavour.

Vanilla

Use the best quality you can afford. Vanilla bean essence is far superior to artificial essence and will give your cakes an intense vanilla flavour.

Tools & equipment

There are a few tools that make cupcake-making easier. Many of these will be in your kitchen already but others, such as piping bags and nozzles, are available from speciality suppliers.

Baking paper

Baking paper – or greaseproof paper – is available at any supermarket.

Cake tins

Line the base and sides of the tin with baking paper before filling with the cake batter. This will make the removal of your cake from the tin and the cleaning of the tin much easier.

Cupcake papers

These are available from most supermarkets in a range of sizes and colours and should be placed inside muffin trays or mini-muffin trays before pouring in the cupcake batter.

Food colouring

Many different brands and types are available from supermarkets and cake-decoration suppliers. Paste colour is intense in hue and is best used for colouring modelling paste and royal icing. Liquid colour may be used for frostings and should be added one drop at a time and thoroughly mixed to gauge the resulting colour before any more is added. Powder colour is best used for colouring white chocolate.

Kitchen scales

There are three types of kitchen scales: balance, spring and digital. Of these, digital scales are definitely the most suitable for baking as they are more convenient to use and far more accurate than the less-expensive spring scales.

Mixers and electric beaters

A set of hand-held electric beaters will make the job of mixing cakes easier. However, a stand mixer, such as KitchenAid, is a good investment if you intend to make a lot of cakes.

Mixing bowls

These are available from most supermarkets and homeware stores. Choose a large sturdy bowl – the extra weight will stop it skidding around when you're mixing.

Muffin trays

These are available from most supermarkets and homeware stores, and come in a range of sizes.

The recipes in this book are all made using a standard 12-hole muffin tray. If you use a different-sized tray be aware this will change the number of cakes you make and the time the cakes take to bake.

Rolling pins

A range of different rolling pins – wooden, plastic, metal, nonstick, silicon and even marble – are available from homeware stores. Personal preference is the best guide: stick with whatever works for you. That said, a heavier pin will save you some effort rolling.

Small utensils

Measuring cups, spoons and jugs are available from homeware stores. Palette knives, small rolling pins and rubber template mats are purchased from specialty cake-decoration suppliers.

Templates, moulds and cutters

Flower cutters, silicon moulds, florists' wire, piping bags and nozzles can be purchased from speciality cake-decoration suppliers. Cutters are available from homeware stores in a range of sizes and shapes and are ideal for making gingerbread shapes and chocolate cut-outs. Make your own templates for cupcake decorations by drawing shapes on a piece of paper in marker pen (or tracing the designs on pages 126–8 onto baking paper). Simply place another piece of baking paper over the top and pipe icing over the pattern that shows through. Leave icing to dry overnight before carefully peeling off the paper and using to decorate your cakes.

How to make a paper piping bag

Steps 1 & 2

Cut a 30cm square piece of baking paper. Cut this in half to form two triangles. Hold one of the triangles in your left hand at the middle of the longest side. Your right hand is holding the point opposite this, the apex of the triangle. Move your right hand over to the right corner and curl it over to the top corner to form a cone.

Steps 3 & 4

Move your left hand to the left corner and roll it around until all corners meet at the top back of the cone. Adjust the shape of the piping bag by sliding the points back and forward between your thumb and fingers until a sharp point is formed at the bottom of the cone.

Step 5

Fold the corners to the inside of the cone, and secure by stapling or tearing each side by the seam and folding the flap inside.

Step 6

Fill the bag by holding it in one hand and using a knife or small spoon. Fold over the opening away from the seam to form a neat seal.

Don't overfill the piping bag – the icing will squeeze out through the top when you are piping, if you do. It should be about half full.

Snip off the point of the piping bag to the thickness you require for piping. It is better to start with a small opening and make it bigger, if necessary.

Holding the bag in your favoured hand, place the point of the bag between your thumb and fingers. Use the thumb to control the flow of the icing. Use the other hand to direct the bag.

It will take practice to master both making and using a piping bag, but the rewards will make the effort worthwhile. Alternatively, you can buy reusable piping bags from specialty suppliers.

Step 1

Step 2

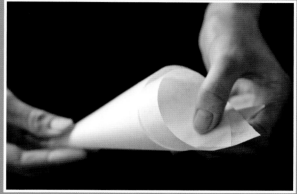

Step 3

Step 4

Step 5

Step 6

Tips for best results

Always preheat the oven.

Begin with well-creamed butter and add the sugar slowly to create good aeration and dissolve the sugar.

Eggs need to be added one at a time to prevent curdling. Beat the mixture well after each addition.

Dry ingredients need to be sifted, especially when adding raising agents to plain flour.

Any additions, such as fruit and nuts, should be added to the mixture after the flour and liquid has been added.

Muffin trays need to be lined with cupcake papers for ease of removal and handling.

Read the recipe instructions thoroughly so you know how many cupcakes the recipe should make. I use standard sized 12-hole muffin trays.

Divide the mixture evenly between the specified number of cupcake papers.

Bake your cakes for the recommended time. (They should spring back when pushed lightly in the centre.)

Cool cupcakes in the muffin trays for five minutes before removing the cupcakes to a wire rack to cool completely.

Cupcakes must be completely cold before icing or decorating.

Cold cupcakes may be stored in an airtight container for up to two days. Un-iced cupcakes can be successfully frozen for up to two weeks, but be sure to defrost completely before decorating.

Cupcake
recipes

Chocolate cupcakes

MAKES 36

430g plain flour

2 teaspoons baking soda

1 teaspoon baking powder

1 teaspoon salt

250ml hot water

100g cocoa

250ml cold water

200g unsalted butter, softened

560g caster sugar

4 eggs

4 teaspoons vanilla essence

Preheat the oven to 170°C. Line three 12-hole muffin trays with cupcake papers.

Sift together the flour, baking soda, baking powder and salt. In a separate bowl whisk together the hot water and cocoa until you have a smooth paste. Add the cold water and whisk until evenly combined.

In a separate bowl, cream the butter for 1–2 minutes. Add the caster sugar and two of the eggs. Beat until light. Add the last two eggs one at a time, beating until well combined, then stir in the vanilla essence. Add half of the flour to the creamed mixture and beat on low speed until combined. Add half of the cocoa mixture and beat until combined. Repeat this process but do not over-beat as this will toughen the mixture.

Divide the mixture between the cupcake papers. They should be about half full as this mixture rises substantially. Bake for 25 minutes or until springy when pressed in the centre.

Cool cupcakes in the muffin trays for 5 minutes before removing the cupcakes to a wire rack to cool completely.

Decoration

Make chocolate frosting (see page 92) and ice the cooled cupcakes. Decorate with chocolate cut-outs (see page 114) and chocolate filigrees (see page 110). Dust with edible gold.

Note: The gold pattern on the chocolate cut-outs in the photograph has been achieved by pouring dark chocolate over a sheet of acetate printed with edible gold pen. When the chocolate hardens and is cut up into the desired shapes, it will have absorbed the designs from the edible pen. Such specialty items are available from selected cake-decoration suppliers.

Mint chocolate cupcakes

MAKES 24

140g dark chocolate

330ml water

4 tablespoons cocoa

300g self-raising flour

⅔ cup ground almonds

180g butter, softened

400g brown sugar

4 eggs

1½ teaspoons peppermint essence

Preheat the oven to 170°C. Line two 12-hole muffin trays with cupcake papers.

Melt the chocolate and water together in a small saucepan, or in a small jug in the microwave. Cool.

Sift the cocoa, flour and ground almonds together.

Beat the butter and sugar until light, then add the eggs one at a time, beating well after each addition. Beat in the peppermint essence.

Stir in the dry ingredients, then the cooled chocolate mix and blend until smooth.

Divide the mixture evenly between the cupcake papers and bake for 30 minutes.

Cool cupcakes in the muffin trays for 5 minutes before removing the cupcakes to a wire rack to cool completely.

Decoration

Make dark chocolate ganache (see page 96) and stir in ½ teaspoon of peppermint essence and mix well. Pipe the ganache onto the cold cupcakes and decorate as desired.

Chocolate and raspberry cupcakes

MAKES 24

120g good quality dark
    chocolate

250ml water

180g butter

220g caster sugar

4 eggs

200g self-raising flour

4 tablespoons cocoa

80g ground almonds

200g fresh or frozen raspberries

Preheat the oven to 170°C. Line two 12-hole muffin trays with cupcake papers.

Combine the chocolate and water in a bowl and place in the microwave on low to melt, or over a pan of simmering water. Stir until smooth.

Cream the butter and sugar with an electric beater until just combined. Gradually add the beaten eggs, beating well after each addition.

Stir in the combined flour, cocoa and ground almonds. Fold in the melted chocolate mixture. Gently stir in the raspberries.

Divide the mixture evenly between the cupcake papers and bake for 30 minutes.

Cool cupcakes in the muffin trays for 5 minutes before removing the cupcakes to a wire rack to cool completely.

Decoration

Make dark chocolate ganache (see page 96) and pipe onto cooled cupcakes. Decorate with pink chocolate filigrees (see page 110) and edible glitter.

Afghan cupcakes

MAKES 24

185g butter

2 teaspoons vanilla essence

380g caster sugar

3 eggs

300g self-raising flour

100g cocoa

250ml water

150g chopped walnuts

Preheat the oven to 175°C. Line two 12-hole muffin trays with cupcake papers.

Place all the ingredients except the walnuts into a large bowl, and using an electric mixer, beat on low speed until just combined. Continue to beat on medium speed until the mixture is smooth and lighter in colour.

Stir in the chopped walnuts.

Divide the mixture between the cupcake papers and bake for 20 minutes, or until the centre of the cake springs back when lightly pressed.

Cool cupcakes in the muffin trays for 5 minutes before removing the cupcakes to a wire rack to cool completely.

Decoration

Make chocolate frosting (see page 92) and ice the cooled cupcakes. Decorate each with caramelised cornflakes (see page 116) and a chocolate spiral (see page 112).

Chocolate banana cupcakes

MAKES 24

450g flour

30g cocoa

2 teaspoons baking powder

2 teaspoons baking soda

60ml milk

225g butter

440g sugar

2 eggs

400g over-ripe bananas, mashed

2 teaspoons vanilla essence

Preheat the oven to 150°C. Line two 12-hole muffin trays with cupcake papers.

Sift the flour, cocoa and baking powder together.

Dissolve the baking soda in the milk.

Cream the butter and sugar until light. Add the eggs one at a time, beating well after each addition. Beat in the sifted flour, cocoa and baking powder, then the mashed bananas, vanilla and milk.

Divide the mixture evenly between the cupcake papers and bake for about 25 minutes.

Cool cupcakes in the muffin trays for 5 minutes before removing the cupcakes to a wire rack to cool completely.

Decoration

Make chocolate frosting (see page 92) and ice the cooled cupcakes. Decorate as desired.

Chocolate cherry cupcakes

MAKES 24

2 x 425g tins pitted cherries in syrup

200g good quality dark chocolate

250g butter

200g caster sugar

300g self-raising flour

4 eggs

Preheat the oven to 170°C. Line two 12-hole muffin trays with cupcake papers.

Drain the cherries and reserve the syrup. Put 1 cup of cherries and 1 cup of syrup into a food processor and process until smooth. Cut the remaining cherries in half and set aside until required. Discard the remaining syrup.

Place the chocolate, butter, sugar and cherry purée into a small saucepan. Stir over a low heat until the chocolate has melted and the mixture is smooth.

Pour into a large bowl to cool for 15 minutes.

Using a whisk, mix in the flour, then the eggs. Stir in the reserved chopped cherries. The mixture will be quite runny.

Divide the mixture evenly between the cupcake papers. Fill each almost to the top as these cakes don't rise very much. Bake for 40 minutes, or until firm to the touch.

Cool cupcakes in the muffin trays for 5 minutes before removing the cupcakes to a wire rack to cool completely.

Decoration

Make dark chocolate ganache (see page 96) and ice the cooled cupcakes. Decorate with chocolate spirals (see page 112).

Chocolate hazelnut cupcakes

MAKES 24

230g butter, softened

220g brown sugar

230g milk chocolate, melted and cooled

2 teaspoons vanilla essence

4 eggs

250g ground hazelnuts

Preheat the oven to 180°C. Line two 12-hole muffin trays with cupcake papers.

Beat the butter in a bowl with electric beaters for 1–2 minutes. Add the brown sugar and continue beating until light and fluffy. Add the cooled melted chocolate and vanilla essence.

Beat in the eggs one at a time, beating well after each addition. Fold in the ground hazelnuts.

Divide the mixture evenly between the cupcake papers and bake for 30 minutes, or until the centre springs back when gently pressed.

Cool cupcakes in the muffin trays for 5 minutes before removing the cupcakes to a wire rack to cool completely.

Decoration

Make chocolate frosting (see page 92) and ice the cooled cupcakes. Decorate each cupcake with three or four caramelised hazelnuts (see caramelised cornflakes variation, page 116) and a toffee filigree. To make the toffee filigree, drizzle some of the caramel used to caramelise the hazelnuts onto baking paper and allow to harden before removing and placing on each cupcake.

Note: For a paler chocolate frosting, simply halve the quantity of cocoa.

White chocolate mud cupcakes

MAKES 36

600g plain flour

2 teaspoons baking powder

500g butter, chopped

500ml milk

900g caster sugar

300g white chocolate, chopped

4 eggs, whisked

2 teaspoons vanilla essence

Preheat the oven to 155°C. Line three 12-hole muffin trays with cupcake papers.

Sift flour and baking powder together into a large bowl. Make a well in the centre and set aside until required.

Put butter, milk, caster sugar and white chocolate into a metal bowl and place over a large saucepan of simmering water. Stir continuously using a flat-bottomed wooden spoon until chocolate has melted and sugar has dissolved. Alternatively, place ingredients into a ceramic bowl and melt in the microwave on high for approximately 5 minutes. Remove from the heat or microwave, and cool to room temperature.

Pour cooled chocolate mixture into the dry ingredients and whisk together until smooth and all lumps are dissolved. Gently stir in the eggs and vanilla essence until just combined.

Divide the mixture evenly between the cupcake papers. They should be two-thirds full. Bake for 30 minutes, or until a fine skewer inserted comes out clean.

Cool cupcakes in the muffin trays for 10 minutes before removing the cupcakes to a wire rack to cool completely.

Decoration

Make white chocolate ganache (see page 96) and pipe onto cooled cupcakes. Decorate with white chocolate triangles (see page 114) and sprinkle with edible glitter flakes.

Note: The pink flecks on the white chocolate triangles in the photograph have been achieved by pouring white chocolate over a decorated acetate sheet. Available from selected cake-decoration suppliers.

Gingerbread cupcakes

MAKES 24

300g plain flour

¼ teaspoon baking soda

½ teaspoon salt

2 tablespoons ground ginger

½ teaspoon mixed spice

150g unsalted butter, softened

400g caster sugar

4 eggs

1½ teaspoons vanilla essence

100g finely chopped crystallised ginger

160ml sour cream

Preheat the oven to 170°C. Line two 12-hole muffin trays with cupcake papers.

Sift together flour, baking soda, salt, ground ginger and mixed spice.

In a separate bowl, cream the butter for 1–2 minutes. Add the caster sugar one-third at a time, beating for 2 minutes after each addition. Beat until the mixture is light and fluffy and the sugar has almost dissolved.

Add eggs one at a time, beating well after each addition until the mixture is light and fluffy. Add the vanilla essence, half the sifted dry ingredients and the chopped ginger and half of the sour cream and stir until just combined. Repeat with the remaining ingredients.

Divide the mixture evenly between the cupcake papers and bake for 20 minutes or until the cakes spring back when gently pressed.

Cool cupcakes in the muffin trays for 5 minutes before removing the cupcakes to a wire rack to cool completely.

Decoration

Make ginger caramel frosting (see page 93) and ice the cooled cupcakes. Decorate with gingerbread hearts (see page 120) and a chocolate filigree (see page 110).

Coconut butter cupcakes

MAKES 36

400g butter, softened

280g caster sugar

2 teaspoons coconut essence

4 eggs

450g self-raising flour

100g desiccated coconut

250ml milk

Preheat the oven to 180°C. Line three 12-hole muffin trays with cupcake papers.

Beat the butter, caster sugar and coconut essence in a bowl until pale and creamy. Add the eggs one at a time and beat well to combine after each addition. Combine flour and coconut in a bowl. Stir into butter mixture alternately with the milk. Mix until just combined.

Divide mixture between the cupcake papers and bake for 12–15 minutes, or until springy when lightly pushed in the middle.

Cool cupcakes in the muffin trays for 5 minutes before removing the cupcakes to a wire rack to cool completely.

Decoration

Make white chocolate ganache (see page 96) and pipe onto cooled cupcakes. Decorate with toasted flaked coconut.

Hokey pokey cupcakes

MAKES 24

415g plain flour

3 teaspoons baking powder

¼ teaspoon salt

230g unsalted butter

230g brown sugar

½ teaspoon vanilla essence

4 eggs

½ cup sour cream

½ cup milk

2 large Cadbury Crunchie bars, crushed

Preheat the oven to 170°C. Line two 12-hole muffin trays with cupcake papers.

Whisk the flour, baking powder and salt together in a small bowl to aerate and combine. Set aside until required.

In a large bowl, use an electric mixer on medium–high speed to beat the butter until creamy, about 2 minutes. Add sugar gradually, beating until light and fluffy, stopping to scrape down the bowl with a spatula once or twice. This will take about 3 minutes. Beat in the vanilla essence. Add eggs one at a time, scraping down the sides of the bowl and beating after each addition.

Combine the sour cream and milk. Add the flour mixture in four additions, alternating with the milk. Begin and end with the flour mixture, and beat briefly until smooth on low speed after each addition. Stir in the crushed chocolate bars.

Divide batter evenly between the cupcake papers and bake for about 18 minutes, or until a toothpick or skewer inserted in the centre shows a few moist crumbs. (The centre should also spring back when lightly pressed.) The cupcakes might colour a bit around the edges, but they will not brown.

Cool cupcakes in the muffin trays for 5 minutes before removing the cupcakes to a wire rack to cool completely.

Decoration

When cold, ice with rich caramel frosting (see page 93) and decorate with the rest of the crushed Cadbury Crunchie bars.

Coffee and pecan cupcakes

MAKES 24

200g self-raising flour

1 teaspoon baking powder

200g butter, softened

230g caster sugar

4 eggs

2 teaspoons vanilla essence

10g instant coffee granules

¼ cup boiling water

125g chopped pecans

Preheat the oven to 170°C. Line two 12-hole muffin trays with cupcake papers.

Sift together the flour and baking powder.

In a separate bowl, cream the butter for 1–2 minutes. Add half the caster sugar and beat for 2 minutes. Add the remaining caster sugar and beat for a further 2 minutes or until the mixture is light and fluffy. Add the eggs one at a time, beating well after each addition or until mixture is light and fluffy. Add the vanilla and beat until combined.

Add half the flour to the creamed mixture and beat on a low speed until combined. Dissolve the coffee in the boiling water. Add the coffee and the remaining flour to the cake mixture and beat until combined, but do not over-beat as this will toughen the mixture. Fold in the chopped pecans.

Divide the mixture evenly between the cupcake papers and bake for 20 minutes.

Cool cupcakes in the muffin trays for 5 minutes before removing the cupcakes to a wire rack to cool completely.

Decoration

Make ginger caramel frosting (see page 93) and ice the cooled cupcakes. Decorate with chocolate cut-outs (see page 114).

Note: The pattern on the chocolate cut-outs in the photograph has been achieved by pouring chocolate over a sheet of printed acetate. Such specialty items are available from selected cake-decoration suppliers.

Date and walnut cupcakes

MAKES 24

250ml golden syrup

60g butter

250ml milk

600g plain flour

220g brown sugar

3 teaspoons baking powder

1 teaspoon baking soda

300g walnut pieces

400g pitted dates, chopped

1 egg, lightly beaten

Preheat the oven to 180°C. Line two 12-hole muffin trays with cupcake papers.

In a saucepan, gently melt the golden syrup, butter and milk together. Do not boil.

Mix the flour, brown sugar, baking powder, baking soda, walnuts and dates together in a bowl and add the egg. Mix together well.

Add the melted golden syrup mixture to the dry ingredients and mix together well.

Divide the mixture evenly between the cupcake papers. They should be two-thirds full. Bake for 18 minutes, or until the tops are firm but springy to touch.

Cool cupcakes in the muffin trays for 5 minutes before removing the cupcakes to a wire rack to cool completely.

Decoration

Make rich caramel frosting (see page 93) and ice the cooled cupcakes. Decorate as desired.

Vanilla cupcakes

MAKES 30

415g plain flour

3 teaspoons baking powder

¼ teaspoon salt

230g unsalted butter, softened

330g sugar

1 tablespoon vanilla essence

4 eggs

250ml milk

Preheat the oven to 170°C. Line two-and-a-half 12-hole muffin trays with cupcake papers.

Whisk flour, baking powder and salt together in a small bowl to aerate and combine. Set aside until required.

In a large bowl, use an electric mixer on medium–high speed to beat butter for about 2 minutes until creamy. Add sugar gradually, beating until light and fluffy, scraping down the bowl once or twice. This will take about 3 minutes. Beat in vanilla essence. Add eggs one at a time, scraping down the sides of the bowl and beating after each addition. Add the flour mixture in four additions, alternately with the milk. Begin and end with the flour mixture, and beat briefly until smooth on a low speed after each addition.

Divide batter evenly between the cupcake papers.

Bake for about 18 minutes, or until a toothpick inserted in the centres shows a few moist crumbs. (The centres should spring back when lightly pressed.) The cupcakes might colour a bit around the edges, but they will not brown.

Cool cupcakes in the muffin trays for 5 minutes before removing the cupcakes to a wire rack to cool completely.

Decoration

Make vanilla frosting (see pages 90 and 94) and ice the cooled cupcakes. Decorate with white lace butterflies (see page 108) and edible glitter.

Spiced vanilla buttermilk cupcakes

MAKES 30

415g plain flour

1 tablespoon baking powder

3 teaspoons mixed spice

1 teaspoon ground cinnamon

½ teaspoon ground cloves

¼ teaspoon ground cardamom

¼ teaspoon salt

230g unsalted butter

330g sugar

3 teaspoons vanilla essence

4 eggs

250ml buttermilk

Preheat the oven to 170°C. Line two-and-a-half 12-hole muffin trays with cupcake papers.

Whisk flour, baking powder, spices and salt together in a small bowl to aerate and combine; then set aside.

In a large bowl, use an electric mixer on medium–high speed to beat butter for about 2 minutes until creamy. Add sugar gradually, beating until light and fluffy, scraping down the bowl once or twice. This will take about 3 minutes. Beat in vanilla essence. Add eggs one at a time, scraping down the sides of the bowl and beating after each addition. Add the flour mixture in two lots, alternately with the buttermilk. Begin and end with the flour mixture, and beat briefly until smooth on a low speed after each addition.

Divide batter evenly between the cupcake papers and bake for about 18 minutes, or until a toothpick inserted in the centre shows a few moist crumbs. (The centre should spring back when lightly pressed.) The cupcakes might colour a bit around the edges, but they will not brown.

Cool cupcakes in the muffin trays for 5 minutes before removing the cupcakes to a wire rack to cool completely.

Decoration

Make vanilla frosting (see pages 90 and 94) and ice the cooled cupcakes. Decorate with lace snowflakes (see pages 108 and 127) and some tiny silver cachous.

Simple butterfly cupcakes

MAKES 24

300g butter, softened

330g caster sugar

4 eggs

2 teaspoons vanilla essence

60ml lemon juice

600g self-raising flour

250ml milk

1 cup jam of your choice

600ml cream

icing sugar to dust

Preheat the oven to 180°C. Line two 12-hole muffin trays with cupcake papers.

Beat the butter and sugar until light and creamy. Add the eggs one at a time, beating well after each addition. Beat in the vanilla essence and lemon juice.

Fold in half the flour, then half the milk. Repeat with the remaining flour and milk. Stir until the mixture is smooth.

Divide the mixture evenly between the muffin trays and bake for 20 minutes, or until the centre springs back when lightly pressed.

Cool cupcakes in the muffin trays for 5 minutes before removing the cupcakes to a wire rack to cool completely.

Decoration

Cut a circle from the top of each cooled cupcake to a depth of about 2cm. Fill the cavity with half a teaspoon of jam.

Whip the cream until stiff peaks form. Spoon or pipe the cream on top of the jam.

Cut each circle of cake in half and place back on the cupcake, angling the pieces to look like wings. Sift a little icing sugar over the cakes to finish.

Ice-cream cone cakes

MAKES 30

30 flat-bottomed ice-cream
cones

180g butter

220g caster sugar

4 eggs

1 teaspoon vanilla essence

300g self-raising flour

4 tablespoons milk

Preheat the oven to 180°C. Place ice-cream cones on a baking tray.

Beat the butter and sugar until light and fluffy. Add the eggs one at a time, beating well after each addition. Mix in the vanilla.

Mix in the flour in two lots alternately with the milk. Beat until a smooth mixture is formed.

Divide the mixture evenly between the cones, taking care not to drop mixture on the outside of the cones as it will burn. The cones should be about half full.

Bake for 15 minutes, or until well risen and springy to touch.

Place the cupcakes on a wire rack to cool completely.

Decoration

Ice with vanilla buttercream frosting (see page 90) and roll in nonpareilles or decorate with cachous.

Rum and raisin cupcakes

MAKES 24

120g raisins

60ml dark rum

600g self-raising flour

60g cocoa

370g butter, softened

330g caster sugar

4 eggs

375ml milk

The night before you want to make the cupcakes, roughly chop the raisins and soak them overnight in the rum.

Preheat the oven to 180°C. Line two 12-hole muffin trays with cupcake papers.

Sift the flour and cocoa together.

Beat the butter and sugar together until light and creamy. Add the eggs one at a time, beating well after each addition.

Fold in the rum-soaked raisins, including any extra rum. Add half the flour and half the milk, and mix to combine. Add the remaining ingredients and stir until the mixture is smooth.

Divide the mixture evenly between the cupcake papers and bake for 20 minutes, or until the centre springs back when lightly pressed.

Cool cupcakes in the muffin trays for 5 minutes before removing the cupcakes to a wire rack to cool completely.

Decoration

Make chocolate frosting (see page 92) and stir in a few drops of rum essence, according to taste. Decorate as desired.

Caramel mud cupcakes

MAKES 36

185g butter, chopped

150g white chocolate, chopped coarsely

220g dark-brown or muscovado sugar

80ml golden syrup

250ml milk

150g plain flour

150g self-raising flour

2 eggs

Preheat the oven to 160°C. Line three 12-hole muffin trays with cupcake papers.

Combine butter, chocolate, sugar, golden syrup and milk in a medium-sized saucepan and stir over a low heat, without boiling, until smooth. Transfer mixture to a large bowl and cool for 15 minutes.

Whisk in sifted flours, then eggs, one at a time. Do not over-mix once the eggs are added.

Divide the mixture evenly between the cupcake cases, and bake for about 25 minutes, or until the centre springs back when lightly pressed.

Cool cupcakes in the muffin trays for 5 minutes before removing the cupcakes to a wire rack to cool completely.

Decoration

Make rich caramel frosting (see page 93) and ice the cooled cupcakes. Decorate with chocolate cut-outs (see page 114).

Light Christmas cupcakes

MAKES 24

100g sultanas

100g currants

100g dried apricots, chopped

125ml brandy

120g plain flour

120g self-raising flour

2 teaspoons mixed spice

240g butter

240g brown sugar

4 eggs

finely grated zest of 2 oranges

The day before you want to cook the cupcakes, soak the sultanas, currants and apricots overnight in the brandy.

Preheat the oven to 170°C. Line two 12-hole muffin tins with cupcake papers.

Sift the flours and mixed spice together and set aside until required.

Beat the butter and sugar with an electric beater until creamy. Add the eggs one at a time, beating after each addition until well combined. Add the orange zest and beat in well. Fold in the soaked dried fruit and flour mixtures with a spoon.

Divide the mixture evenly between the cupcake papers and bake for about 25 minutes.

Cool cupcakes in the muffin trays for 5 minutes before removing the cupcakes to a wire rack to cool completely.

Decoration

Brush the top of each cooled cupcake with boiled apricot jam. Decorate with a circle of rolled fondant and two glitter Christmas trees using modelling paste (see page 101).

Banana cupcakes

MAKES 24

180g butter, softened

220g brown sugar

4 eggs

150g self-raising flour

150g plain flour

1 teaspoon baking soda

1 teaspoon ground cinnamon

400g over-ripe bananas, mashed

160g sour cream

60ml milk

Preheat the oven to 180°C. Line two 12-hole muffin trays with cupcake papers.

Beat the butter and sugar in a small bowl until light and fluffy. Add the eggs one at a time, beating well after each addition.

Stir in sifted dry ingredients, then bananas, sour cream and milk.

Divide mixture evenly between the cupcake papers and bake for 25 minutes.

Cool cupcakes in the muffin trays for 5 minutes before removing the cupcakes to a wire rack to cool completely.

Decoration

Make cream cheese frosting (see page 95) and ice the cooled cupcakes. Decorate with bright daisies (see page 106) and white chocolate filigrees (see page 110).

Almond and lime cupcakes

MAKES 24

600g self-raising flour

200g ground almonds

250g butter, softened

350g caster sugar

4 eggs

250ml milk

finely grated zest and juice
of 2 limes

Preheat the oven to 180°C. Line two 12-hole muffin trays with cupcake papers.

Stir the flour and almonds together to aerate and set aside until required.

Beat the butter and caster sugar together until light and creamy. Add the eggs one at a time, beating well after each addition, until the mixture is fluffy. Fold in the flour and almonds, then the milk and lime zest and juice.

Divide the mixture evenly between the cupcake papers and bake for 30 minutes, or until the centre springs back when gently pressed.

Cool cupcakes in the muffin trays for 5 minutes before removing the cupcakes to a wire rack to cool completely.

Decoration

Make a lemon or lime frosting (see page 92, variation) and ice the cooled cupcakes. Decorate as desired.

Passionfruit butter cupcakes

MAKES 24

230g self-raising flour

230g butter

230g caster sugar

4 eggs

6 passionfruit, halved

finely grated zest of 1 lemon

Preheat the oven to 180°C. Line two 12-hole muffin trays with cupcake papers.

Sift the flour to aerate and set aside until required.

Beat the butter and sugar together in a bowl with electric beaters until light. Add the eggs one at a time, beating well after each addition. Fold in the flour alternately with the passionfruit pulp. Stir in the lemon zest.

Divide the mixture between the cupcake papers and bake for 15 minutes.

Cool cupcakes in the muffin trays for 5 minutes before removing the cupcakes to a wire rack to cool completely.

Decoration

Make passionfruit frosting (see page 90) and ice the cooled cupcakes. Decorate as desired.

Carrot cupcakes

MAKES 30

560g self-raising flour

2 teaspoons baking soda

1 teaspoon mixed spice

500ml vegetable oil

520g brown sugar

6 eggs

600g carrot, peeled and grated

150g chopped pecans

125g sultanas

finely grated zest of 2 lemons

Preheat the oven to 180°C. Line two-and-a-half 12-hole muffin trays with cupcake papers.

Sift together the flour, baking soda and mixed spice. In a separate bowl, beat the vegetable oil, brown sugar and eggs together for about 5 minutes or until thick and creamy.

Add the grated carrot, pecans, sultanas and lemon zest. Beat on a low speed until combined.

Add the flour mixture and beat until thoroughly combined, but do not over-beat as this will toughen the mixture.

Divide mixture evenly between the cupcake papers and bake for 25 minutes.

Cool cupcakes in the muffin trays for 5 minutes before removing the cupcakes to a wire rack to cool completely.

Decoration

Make cream cheese frosting (see page 95) and ice the cooled cupcakes. Decorate with mini carrots using modelling paste (see page 101).

Orange and poppy seed cupcakes

**MAKES 24 CUPCAKES
OR 16 MINI LOAVES**

300g plain flour

3 teaspoons baking powder

250g butter

finely grated zest of 2 oranges

225g caster sugar

4 eggs

250g ground almonds

2 tablespoons poppy seeds

½ cup milk

½ cup orange juice

Preheat the oven to 180°C. Line two 12-hole muffin trays with cupcake papers.

Sift the flour and baking powder together into a bowl to aerate. Set aside until required.

Place butter, zest and sugar in a bowl and mix until light and creamy. Add eggs one at a time, beating after each addition until combined.

Stir through ground almonds and poppy seeds. Stir in half the flour and half the milk, then the remaining flour, milk and juice.

Divide mixture evenly between the cupcake papers and bake for 25 minutes.

Cool cupcakes in the muffin trays for 5 minutes before removing the cupcakes to a wire rack to cool completely.

Decoration

Make orange frosting (see page 92) and ice the cooled cupcakes. Decorate as desired.

Lemon cupcakes

MAKES 30

415g plain flour

3 teaspoons baking powder

¼ teaspoon salt

230g unsalted butter, softened

330g sugar

½ teaspoon lemon essence

4 eggs

½ cup sour cream

½ cup milk

Preheat the oven to 170°C. Line two-and-a-half 12-hole muffin trays with cupcake papers.

Whisk flour, baking powder and salt together in a small bowl to aerate and combine. Set aside until required.

In a large bowl, use an electric mixer on medium–high speed to beat butter until creamy, about 2 minutes. Add sugar gradually, beating until light and fluffy, scraping down the bowl once or twice. This will take about 3 minutes. Beat in lemon essence. Add eggs one at a time, scraping down the sides of the bowl and beating after each addition.

Mix the sour cream and milk together. Add the flour mixture in four additions, alternating with the milk mixture. Begin and end with the flour mixture, and beat briefly until smooth on low speed after each addition.

Divide batter evenly between the cupcake papers, and bake for about 18 minutes, or until a toothpick inserted in the centre shows a few moist crumbs. (The centre should spring back when lightly pressed.) The cupcakes might colour a bit around the edges, but they will not brown.

Cool cupcakes in the muffin trays for 5 minutes before removing the cupcakes to a wire rack to cool completely.

Decoration

Use a melon-ball scoop and cut out a circle of cake from the centre of each cupcake. Fill with lemon curd (see page 95) and top with a meringue (see page 118) and a bright daisy (see page 106).

Apple and cinnamon cupcakes

MAKES 24

juice of 2 large lemons

2 eating apples of your choice, peeled, cored and chopped into very fine pieces

220g caster sugar

220g butter

4 eggs

350g self-raising flour

1 teaspoon ground cinnamon

Preheat the oven to 190°C. Line two 12-hole muffin trays with cupcake papers.

Squeeze the lemons and set 2 tablespoons of juice aside until required. Pour the rest of the juice over the chopped apple to prevent the apple going brown.

Beat together the sugar and butter. Add the eggs one at a time and beat well after each addition. Add 2 tablespoons of lemon juice. Add the flour and cinnamon, and mix together.

Put 2 tablespoons of mixture into each cupcake paper. Divide the chopped apple evenly between the cupcakes and place on top of the cake mixture. Top with the remaining mixture.

Bake for 20 minutes, or until the centre springs back when lightly pressed.

Cool cupcakes in the muffin trays for 5 minutes before removing the cupcakes to a wire rack to cool completely.

Decoration

Make passionfruit frosting or lemon buttercream frosting (see page 90) and decorate with thinly sliced apple and edible glitter. To make the stripes in the apple, use a vegetable peeler to remove a stripe of peel from around the apple in a spiral before slicing thinly and placing on the cupcakes.

Hummingbird cupcakes

MAKES 36

250g plain flour

125g self-raising flour

1 teaspoon baking soda

1 teaspoon mixed spice

2 x 450g tins crushed pineapple in juice, drained (reserve 125ml juice)

400g soft brown sugar

80g desiccated coconut

400g over-ripe bananas, mashed

4 eggs, whisked

325ml vegetable oil

Preheat the oven to 170°C. Line three 12-hole muffin trays with cupcake papers.

In a very large bowl sift together flours, baking soda and mixed spice. Add the remaining ingredients, including reserved pineapple juice and mix together using a large rubber spatula. Stir until evenly combined.

Divide mixture evenly between the cupcake papers. They should be about three-quarters full. Bake for 25 minutes or until a fine skewer inserted comes out clean.

Cool cupcakes in the muffin trays for 5 minutes before removing the cupcakes to a wire rack to cool completely.

Decoration

Make cream cheese frosting (see page 95) and ice the cooled cupcakes. Decorate with butterflies and colour co-ordinated bright daisies (see page 106).

Fat-free fruit and spice cupcakes

MAKES 24

4 Sanitarium Weet-Bix, crumbled

200g mixed dried fruit

330g brown sugar

600ml non-fat milk

600g self-raising flour

2 eggs, lightly beaten

1 teaspoon mixed spice

½ teaspoon baking powder

The day before you want to cook the cupcakes, soak the Weet-Bix, dried fruit and sugar in the milk.

Preheat the oven to 190°C. Line two 12-hole muffin trays with cupcake papers.

Add the flour, eggs, mixed spice and baking powder to the soaked fruit mixture and mix together gently.

Divide the mixture evenly between the cupcake papers. They should be two-thirds full. Bake in the oven for 20 minutes, or until a skewer inserted in the centre comes out clean.

Cool cupcakes in the muffin trays for 5 minutes before removing the cupcakes to a wire rack to cool completely.

Decoration

These are best eaten warm, but if you want to serve them cold they are nice iced with a little lemon buttercream frosting (see page 90).

Dairy-free strawberry cupcakes

MAKES 36

220g soy or olive spread, or other dairy-free alternative of your choice

2 teaspoons vanilla essence

330g caster sugar

450g self-raising flour

2 eggs

375ml water

200g chopped fresh or frozen strawberries

Preheat the oven to 180°C. Line three 12-hole muffin trays with cupcakes papers.

Place the spread, vanilla essence, sugar, flour, eggs and water into a bowl and, using an electric mixer on low speed, beat for 1 minute until blended.

Increase speed to high. Beat for a further 4 minutes or until mixture has thickened. Stir in the chopped berries.

Divide the mixture evenly between the cupcake papers and bake for 12–15 minutes, or until golden brown.

Cool cupcakes in the muffin trays for 5 minutes before removing the cupcakes to a wire rack to cool completely.

Decoration

Make dairy-free vanilla frosting (see page 94) and ice the cooled cupcakes. Decorate with hearts sprinkled with edible glitter (see page 102).

Gluten-free blueberry cupcakes

MAKES 24

300g ground almonds

400g icing sugar, sifted

200g gluten-free plain flour

finely grated zest of 1 lemon

10 egg whites, at room temperature

300g butter, melted and cooled

300g fresh or frozen blueberries

Preheat the oven to 200°C. Line two 12-hole muffin trays with cupcake papers.

Place almonds, sugar, flour and lemon zest into a bowl. Mix well to combine and set aside until required.

In a separate bowl, whisk egg whites with a fork until frothy. Add to flour mixture. Mix until just combined. Stir in melted butter and gently fold through the berries.

Divide the mixture evenly between the cupcake papers. They should be three-quarters full. Bake for 20 minutes, or until a skewer inserted into the centre comes out clean.

Cool cupcakes in the muffin trays for 10 minutes before removing the cupcakes to a wire rack to cool completely.

Decoration

Make cream cheese frosting (see page 95) and ice the cooled cupcakes. Decorate with bright daisies on wires (see pages 102 and 106).

Gluten-free chocolate cupcakes

MAKES 24

100g dark chocolate

130g rice flour

80g gluten-free cornflour

65g potato flour

75g cocoa

2 teaspoons gluten-free baking powder

1 teaspoon baking soda

2 eggs, at room temperature

330g caster sugar

50g butter, melted

200g gluten-free vanilla yoghurt

160ml reduced-fat milk

1 teaspoon vanilla essence

Preheat the oven to 170°C. Line two 12-hole muffin trays with cupcake papers.

Melt the chocolate in the microwave or in a bowl over simmering water. Allow to cool slightly.

Sift flours, cocoa, baking powder and baking soda into a large bowl.

Whisk the eggs and sugar in a bowl. Add the butter, yoghurt, milk and vanilla. Mix well. Pour egg mixture into flour mixture. Using an electric mixer, beat on low for 2 minutes or until mixture is pale in colour. Mix in the melted chocolate.

Divide the mixture evenly between the cupcake papers. They should only be about half full as these cupcakes rise a lot. Bake for 18 minutes.

Cool cupcakes in the muffin trays for 5 minutes before removing the cupcakes to a wire rack to cool completely.

Decoration

Make dairy-free chocolate frosting (see page 94) and ice the cooled cupcakes. Decorate as desired.

Gluten-free sticky date cupcakes *(with dairy-free option)*

MAKES 24

400g chopped dates

700ml water

2 teaspoons vanilla essence

4 teaspoons baking soda

180g butter (or dairy-free spread for dairy-free option)

220g dark-brown or muscovado sugar

4 eggs, lightly whisked

400g gluten-free flour

Preheat the oven to 180°C. Line two 12-hole muffin trays with cupcake papers.

Place dates and water in a medium-sized saucepan and cook for 5 minutes or until soft. Stir in vanilla essence and baking soda. Allow to cool.

Beat together butter or spread, if using, and sugar until pale and creamy. Gradually add eggs. Stir in cooled date mixture. Fold in the flour.

Divide the mixture between the cupcake papers and bake for 20–25 minutes, or until cupcakes spring back when pressed.

Cool cupcakes in the muffin trays for 5 minutes before removing the cupcakes to a wire rack to cool completely.

Decoration

Make rich caramel frosting (see page 93) and ice the cooled cupcakes. Decorate as desired.

Gluten-free orange and almond cupcakes

MAKES 24

130g gluten-free plain flour

1 teaspoon gluten-free baking powder

250g butter

finely grated zest of 2 oranges

225g caster sugar

4 eggs

250g ground almonds

125ml milk

½ cup orange juice

Preheat the oven to 180°C. Line two 12-hole muffin trays with cupcake papers.

Sift the flour and baking power together into a bowl and set aside until required.

Place butter, zest and sugar in a bowl and mix until light and creamy. Add eggs one at a time, beating after each addition until combined.

Stir ground almonds, half the flour and half the milk into the mixture until combined. Add the remaining flour and milk, and stir through.

Divide the mixture evenly between the cupcake papers and bake for 20 minutes.

Cool cupcakes in the muffin trays for 5 minutes before removing the cupcakes to a wire rack to cool completely.

Decoration

Make orange frosting (see page 92) and ice the cooled cupcakes. Decorate each with an orange open rose (see page 104).

Celebration
cakes

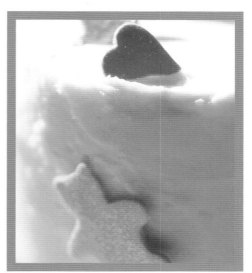

Chocolate mud cake with chocolate collar and gold stars

225g self-raising flour

150g plain flour

45g cocoa

250g butter

200g dark chocolate

330g caster sugar

1 tablespoon vegetable or canola oil

10g instant coffee powder

250ml water

2 eggs

Preheat the oven to 160°C. Line the base and sides of a 16cm round cake tin with baking paper.

Sift the flours and cocoa into a bowl. Melt the butter, chocolate, sugar, oil, coffee and water together in a separate bowl in the microwave. Stir until smooth. Pour into dry ingredients and mix well with a whisk. Add the eggs and stir to just combine – do not over-beat.

Spoon mixture into prepared tin and bake for 1½ hours, or until cake is soft but cooked in the centre. Place on a wire rack and allow to cool in the tin overnight.

When cold, remove from the tin, peel off the baking paper and place on a cake board.

Decoration

Make chocolate frosting (see page 92) or dark chocolate ganache (see page 96). When thickened and cool, use a palette knife to spread all over the cake.

Cut a strip of baking paper long enough to circle the cake. Cut the width to just above the height of the cake. Melt 150g dark chocolate and spread over the baking paper to a thickness of about 1mm. Working quickly, pick up the paper and wrap it around the cake. Make sure the ends meet neatly.

Allow the chocolate to set before peeling away the paper.

Make gold stars on wires (see page 102) and chocolate spirals (see page 112) and place randomly over the cake.

White chocolate and raspberry mud cake

300g plain flour

¾ teaspoon baking powder

450g caster sugar

250g butter

150g white chocolate buttons

250ml milk

2 eggs

1 teaspoon vanilla essence

150g frozen raspberries

Preheat the oven to 160°C. Line the base and sides of a 16cm round cake tin with baking paper.

Sift the flour and baking powder together into a bowl. Melt the sugar, butter, chocolate and milk together in a separate bowl in the microwave. Stir until smooth. Pour into dry ingredients and mix well with a whisk. Add the eggs and vanilla and stir to just combine – do not over-beat. Gently stir through the raspberries.

Spoon mixture into prepared tin and bake for 1½ hours, or until cake is soft but cooked in the centre. Place on a wire rack and allow to cool in the tin overnight.

When cold, remove from the tin, peel off the baking paper and place on a cake board.

Decoration

Make white chocolate ganache (see page 96). When thickened and cool, use a palette knife to spread ganache all over the cake.

Make pale lemon-tinted lace butterflies (see page 108) and place the butterflies randomly over the cake top. Finish with a sprinkle of edible glitter.

Lemon sour cream butter cake

150g plain flour

2 tablespoons self-raising flour

125g butter, softened

220g caster sugar

1 teaspoon finely grated lemon
    zest

3 eggs

100g sour cream

Preheat the oven to 165°C. Line the base and sides of a 16cm round cake tin with baking paper.

Sift the flours together and set aside until required.

Cream the butter, sugar and lemon zest until light and fluffy. Add the eggs one at a time, beating well after each addition.

Stir in half the flour and half the sour cream, then stir in the remaining flour and sour cream. Stir until the mixture is smooth.

Spread the mixture in the prepared tin and bake for about 45 minutes, or until a skewer inserted into the centre comes out clean.

Allow to cool in the tin for 10 minutes before turning onto a wire rack to finish cooling.

Remove the paper and place the cake on a board.

Decoration

Make lemon buttercream frosting (see page 90, variation). Using a palette knife, spread the frosting over the cake.

Make different sizes of yellow and white daisies on wires (see pages 102 and 106). Attach the daisies to lengths of florists' wire and push the wires into the centre of the cake. Finish with a sprinkle of edible glitter.

Vanilla cake with vanilla frosting and glitter teddies

125g butter
185ml milk
3 eggs
1 tablespoon vanilla essence
220g caster sugar
225g self-raising flour

Preheat the oven to 180°C. Line the base and sides of a 16cm round cake tin with baking paper.

Place the butter and milk in a small saucepan over medium heat. Stir constantly until the butter is melted. Remove from the heat and leave to cool to room temperature. Alternatively, place the butter and milk in a heatproof jug and microwave on high until the butter is melted. Leave to cool.

Using electric beaters, beat the eggs and vanilla until thick and foamy. Gradually add the sugar, beating after each addition until the sugar has dissolved.

Stir in half the flour, then half the cooled butter mixture. Repeat with the remaining ingredients.

Pour into the prepared tin and bake for 45 minutes, or until a skewer inserted into the centre comes out clean.

Allow to cool in the tin for 5 minutes before turning onto a wire rack to finish cooling.

Remove the paper and place the cake on a board.

Decoration

Make vanilla buttercream frosting (see page 90).
Using a palette knife, spread frosting all over the cake.

Make some small cut-out teddies or other shapes from modelling paste (see page 101). Allow to dry, brush lightly with sugar syrup and sprinkle with edible glitter then place randomly on the cake.

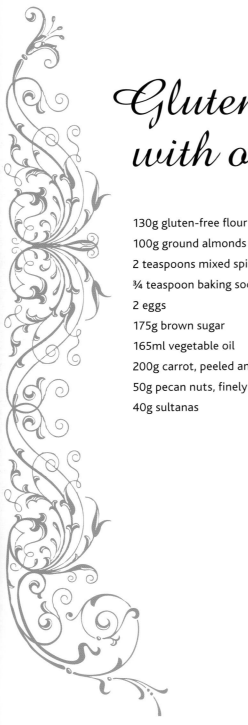

Gluten-free carrot cake with orange frosting

130g gluten-free flour

100g ground almonds

2 teaspoons mixed spice

¾ teaspoon baking soda

2 eggs

175g brown sugar

165ml vegetable oil

200g carrot, peeled and grated

50g pecan nuts, finely chopped

40g sultanas

Preheat the oven to 180°C. Line the base and sides of a 16cm round cake tin with baking paper.

Sift together the flour, almonds, mixed spice and baking soda and set aside until required.

Using electric beaters, whisk the eggs, sugar and oil together in a bowl until the mixture is thick and creamy.

Stir in the grated carrot, nuts and sultanas, then the flour mixture. Stir until well combined.

Pour mix into the prepared tin and bake for 35 minutes, or until a skewer inserted into the centre comes out with only a few crumbs.

Allow to cool in the tin for 5 minutes before turning onto a wire rack to finish cooling.

Remove the paper and place the cake on a board.

Decoration

Make pale orange-tinted vanilla buttercream frosting (see page 90). Using a palette knife, spread the frosting over the cake.

Make multi-coloured hearts on wires (see page 102) and bright daisies (see page 106) and place on the cake top and sides.

Fruitcake

250g sultanas

125g raisins

60g currants

60g mixed peel

30g glacé cherries, chopped

30g natural almonds, chopped

60ml sherry or brandy

2 teaspoons glycerine

125g plain flour

30g self-raising flour

½ teaspoon ground nutmeg

½ teaspoon ground cinnamon

½ teaspoon mixed spice

125g butter, softened

125g brown sugar

2 teaspoons marmalade

3 eggs

apricot jam

almond-flavoured fondant

white fondant

The day before you want to make the cake, mix the dried fruits and nuts together in a bowl and pour over the sherry or brandy and glycerine. Stir through, cover and leave for at least 24 hours.

Preheat the oven to 160°C. Line the base and sides of a 16cm round cake tin with baking paper.

Sift together the flours and spices.

Beat the butter and sugar until just beginning to cream. Add the marmalade and eggs slowly to prevent the mixture curdling.

Stir half the soaked fruit and half the flour mix into the batter. Repeat with the remaining ingredients.

Spoon the mixture into the prepared tin, smooth the top with the spoon making an indent in the centre and the sides of the cake higher. Bake for 20 minutes at 160°C, then reduce the heat to 130°C and bake for 2 hours.

Place on a wire rack and allow to cool in the tin overnight. When cold, remove from the tin and wrap in foil until ready to use.

When ready to decorate, remove the foil and place the cake top side down on a board.

Decoration

Brush the cake with warmed apricot jam or homemade sugar syrup (see page 102).

Roll out purchased almond-flavoured fondant in a circle, large enough to cover the cake. Smooth down over the cake with your hand. Using a knife, trim away the excess fondant from around the base of the cake. Allow to dry overnight.

Roll out purchased white fondant icing in a circle, large enough

to cover the cake completely. Brush the cake with sugar syrup.
Place the fondant over the cake and smooth down over the cake
with your hand. Using a knife, trim away the excess fondant from
around the base of the cake. Allow to dry overnight.

The cake is ready to be decorated as desired. A ribbon around
the side is a neat way to finish this cake. Hand-made white open
roses (see page 104) or purchased large roses are another simple
way to present this cake.

Toppings & frostings

Passionfruit frosting

125g butter, softened

500g icing sugar

4 passionfruit

1 teaspoon lemon juice

Beat the butter in a bowl with electric beaters until creamy. Add half the icing sugar and the pulp of two passionfruit. Beat until the mixture is light and creamy, and begins to increase in volume. Add the remaining icing sugar, passionfruit pulp and the lemon juice, and continue beating until light and creamy.

Vanilla buttercream frosting

200g unsalted butter, softened

125ml milk

1 tablespoon vanilla essence

2kg icing sugar, sifted

Cream the butter for 1–2 minutes. Add the milk, vanilla and half the icing sugar. Beat for at least 3 minutes, or until the mixture is light and fluffy. Add the remaining icing sugar and beat for a further 3 minutes, or until the mixture is of a spreadable consistency. If the mixture is too dry, add extra milk; and if the mixture is too wet, add extra icing sugar.

If you wish to colour and/or flavour the buttercream, then this is the time to do it. Add a drop at a time until you reach the desired colour and/or flavour.

Variations

Coffee buttercream: Add 2 tablespoons of instant coffee dissolved in ¼ cup boiling water. Use ¼ cup of milk and the coffee mixture instead of ½ cup milk to make the buttercream.

Lemon buttercream: Add 1 tablespoon of grated lemon zest and 2 tablespoons of lemon juice to the creamed butter. Then continue as per the recipe, omitting the vanilla.

Toppings and frostings **91**

Chocolate frosting

250g butter, softened

500g icing sugar

⅔ cup cocoa

125ml milk

2 teaspoons vanilla essence

Beat the butter with electric beaters until well softened. Add half the icing sugar, half the cocoa and half the milk. Beat until light and fluffy. Scrape down the bowl and add the remaining ingredients. Beat again until the mixture is light and smooth. If the frosting is too stiff add a little more milk.

Orange frosting

200g unsalted butter, softened

1.5kg icing sugar

finely grated zest and juice
   of 1 orange

80ml milk

Beat the butter with half the icing sugar, orange zest and juice. Continue to beat until the mixture is light and fluffy. Add the remaining icing sugar and milk and continue beating until the mixture is light and fluffy.

Variation

Replace orange zest and juice with the zest and juice of two lemons or limes if desired.

Rich caramel frosting

100g butter

125g brown or muscovado
  sugar

75g golden syrup

125ml cream

1kg icing sugar

Combine the butter, sugar, golden syrup and cream in a heavy-based saucepan over a medium heat. Stir occasionally with a flat-bottomed wooden spoon until the sugar has dissolved. Turn heat up to high and boil for at least 5 minutes. Take off the heat and cool to room temperature.

Add half of the sifted icing sugar to the cooled caramel mixture and use an electric mixer on medium speed to beat for 3 minutes or until the mixture is light and fluffy. Add the remaining icing sugar and beat for a further 3 minutes or until the mixture is of a spreadable consistency. If the mixture is too dry, add extra cream; and if the mixture is too wet, add extra icing sugar.

Ginger caramel frosting

125g butter

200g brown sugar

80ml cream

1 tablespoon ground ginger

500g icing sugar

Melt the butter in a small saucepan. Add the brown sugar and stir over a low heat until the sugar dissolves. Bring the mix to a boil, reduce heat and cook for 2–3 minutes. Stir in the cream and ginger.

Cool to a lukewarm temperature. Gradually stir in the icing sugar and cool the mixture completely. Beat until the frosting is light and creamy. If the frosting is too stiff, add a little more cream.

Dairy-free chocolate frosting

125g soy or olive spread, or other dairy-free alternative of your choice

500g icing sugar

80g cocoa

100ml soy or rice milk

2 teaspoons vanilla essence

Beat the spread in a bowl with electric beaters until creamy. Add half the icing sugar and cocoa, and 2 tablespoons of the milk. Beat until the icing begins to get lighter in colour and increases in volume. Add the remaining icing sugar, cocoa, milk and the vanilla. Beat again until all the ingredients are well combined and the mixture is very creamy. If the frosting is too stiff, add a little more milk.

Dairy-free vanilla frosting

200g soy or olive spread, or other dairy-free alternative of your choice

600g icing sugar

80ml soy or rice milk

2 teaspoons vanilla essence

50ml vanilla soy yogurt

In a large mixing bowl using an electric hand mixer, cream the spread for about 2 minutes until fluffy.

Add the icing sugar gradually, beating at a low speed until combined.

Turn up the speed to high and beat in the milk, vanilla and yoghurt. Continue to beat until the mixture is smooth and creamy.

Chill slightly before use.

Cream cheese frosting

125g unsalted butter, softened

400g cream cheese, softened

2 teaspoons lemon juice

6 cups icing sugar, sifted

Cream the butter for 1–2 minutes. Add the cream cheese, lemon juice and half of the sifted icing sugar and beat for 3 minutes or until the mixture is light and fluffy. Gradually add remaining icing sugar and beat until the mixture is light and of a spreadable consistency. You can use the frosting immediately or store it in an airtight container in the fridge for up to 1 week.

Lemon curd

4 egg yolks

75g caster sugar

2 teaspoons finely grated lemon zest

60ml lemon juice

40g butter

Combine ingredients in a small heatproof bowl over a small saucepan of simmering water, stirring constantly, until mixture thickens slightly and coats the back of a spoon. Remove from heat and allow to cool. Store in an airtight container in the fridge for up to 4 weeks.

Chocolate ganache

DARK CHOCOLATE GANACHE

400g dark chocolate

375ml cream

WHITE CHOCOLATE GANACHE

600g white chocolate

250ml cream

Melt the chocolate and cream together over a saucepan of gently simmering water or in the microwave on low power. Stir to combine and set aside to cool before use.

Royal icing

1 egg white

300g icing sugar, sifted

½ teaspoon lemon juice

Beat the egg white in a small bowl with electric beaters until foamy. Gradually add the sugar a spoonful at a time, beating well after each addition. The icing is ready when peaks appear and hold their shape. Beat in the lemon juice.

Cover the bowl with plastic wrap until required.

Using a fine nozzle, pipe the royal icing onto silicon paper to make butterflies, snowflakes and delicate decorations for cakes. The icing will harden when dry and can be easily lifted off the silicon paper.

Variation

The icing can be coloured as desired, but the addition of liquid colourings will cause the icing to become runny. Paste colour is more suitable.

Decorations

Gum paste

- 625g icing sugar
- 75g cornflour
- 3 teaspoons gum tragacanth
- 5 teaspoons cold water
- 2 teaspoons gelatine
- 2 teaspoons glucose syrup
- 3 teaspoons white vegetable shortening
- 1 large egg white

Sift icing sugar and cornflour into the bowl of an electric mixer. Sprinkle gum tragacanth on top. Set the bowl in a pan of boiling water and cover with a cloth.

Put the water and gelatine in the top of a double boiler and allow the gelatine to soften for 5 minutes.

Bring the water in the bottom of the double boiler to a simmer. Set the gelatine mixture on top and add the glucose and shortening to the gelatine mixture. Stir until the shortening is completed melted.

Pour the gelatine mixture into the icing sugar mixture and beat on low speed until all ingredients are combined. Continue to beat on high speed for 5–10 minutes, or until the dough looks stringy.

Wrap the gum paste in plastic wrap or place in an airtight plastic bag and refrigerate for 24 hours.

After it sits in the fridge the gum paste will become stiff. Knead it a little so the warmth of your hands soften it. Add a dab of shortening and work it into the gum paste to make it pliable, if required. It dries quickly when exposed to air, so only remove what you need from the plastic.

Roll the gum paste out on a greased surface or dust the surface and rolling pin with cornflour to prevent sticking.

Use only paste food colour to tint gum paste. Add a tiny amount at a time, using a toothpick. Knead the colour into the gum paste until the colour is uniform throughout. Some colours tend to darken over time, so tint the gum paste slightly lighter than the desired colour. After you add colour, you may find that the gum paste becomes too soft. If that happens, allow it to sit for 15 minutes and it will return to its normal texture.

Roll out thinly to make leaves, butterflies and petals for flowers.

Modelling paste

500g icing sugar

130g cornflour

110ml water

1½ tablespoons gelatine

1 teaspoon cream of tartar

Sift the icing sugar and cornflour into a large mixing bowl to combine.

Place the water, gelatine and cream of tartar in a glass measuring jug and allow to stand for 5 minutes. Place the jug in the microwave and heat on low in 10 second bursts until the gelatine has dissolved. Be careful not to overheat the mixture. If you do not have a microwave, place the water, gelatine and cream of tartar in a bowl. Allow to stand for 5 minutes and then heat gently over a pan of simmering water until the gelatine dissolves.

Pour the gelatine mixture into the bowl with the cornflour and icing sugar. Mix thoroughly until well combined. Allow to rest in the bowl, covered with a damp towel for an hour. Place the paste into an airtight container and store in the fridge until required. This paste is best left overnight before making decorations. It can also be frozen for up to 1 month if desired – allow to defrost in the fridge before use.

This recipe is great for making icing butterflies and three-dimensional decorations, such as hearts and stars on wires (see page 102).

Sugar syrup

125ml water

110g sugar

1 teaspoon glucose syrup

Combine the ingredients in a small saucepan. Stir over low heat without boiling, until the sugar dissolves. Bring to the boil, reduce to a simmer and cook the syrup for 5 minutes.

Allow to cool. Store in an airtight jar for up to 2 weeks.

Use as glue for sticking wires into cut shapes, or glitter onto shapes.

Hearts and stars on wires

paste food colouring

modelling paste (see page 101)

cornflour

egg white, lightly beaten

wire snips

24-gauge florists' wire

rolling pin

heart or star cutter

Using the wire snips, cut the florists' wire into the lengths you need. Knead a small amount of paste colouring into the modelling paste. Use cornflour on your hands and work surface to stop the paste sticking. Once you have the desired colour, roll out the paste to a thickness of about 3mm. Using a small heart or star cutter, cut out the number of shapes required. Dip the end of the wire into the egg white and then push gently into the shapes. Place onto a tray that has been lined with baking paper and dusted with cornflour, and allow to dry overnight.

When dry, the shapes can be decorated with piped royal icing (see page 96), or brushed with sugar syrup and sprinkled with edible glitter.

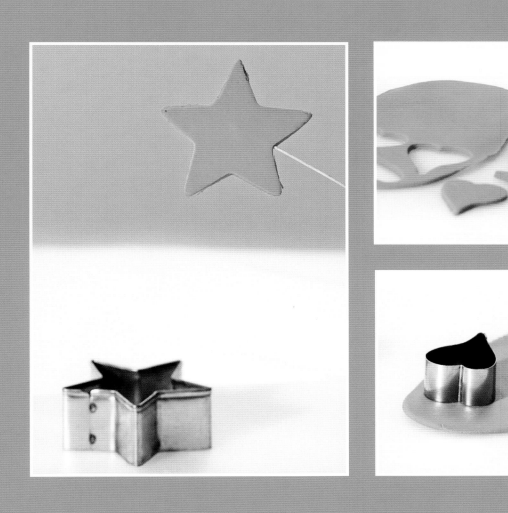

Orange open roses

orange food colouring paste

modelling paste (see page 101)

cornflour

royal icing (see page 96)

yellow nonpareilles

toothpick

rolling pin

small rose cutter

piece of thick sponge

round ball modelling tool

baking paper

patty pan tin

Using a toothpick, add a small amount of orange food colouring to the modelling paste and knead until uniform in colour. Dust the work surface with cornflour and roll out a piece of paste until it is very thin. You should be able to see through it.

Using the rose cutter, press out five petals for each flower. Gently thin the curved top of the petal between your thumb and fingers.

Place the petals on the piece of sponge and gently press the centre of the petal with the round ball modelling tool to flute and cup it. Place each petal on a tray lined with baking paper and allow to dry overnight.

Cut small squares of baking paper about 1cm in size. Place one in each indent in a patty pan tray.

Make a paper piping bag (see page 14) and half fill with white royal icing (see page 96).

Pipe a mound of icing in the middle of each square of baking paper. Lay five petals in the icing, overlapping each to form a flower shape. Pipe another small mound of icing in the centre of the flower and gently press a few yellow nonpareilles into the icing.

Allow to dry. Remove from the baking paper and use to decorate immediately or store in an airtight container for up to 3 months.

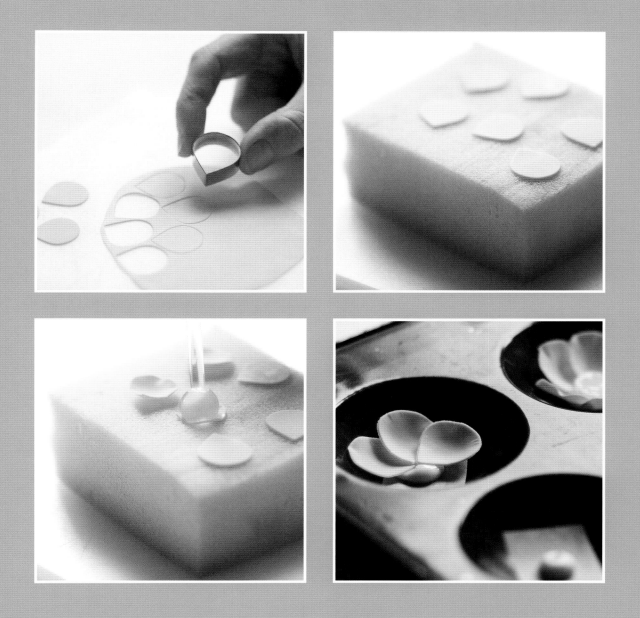

Butterflies and bright daisies

food paste colouring

modelling paste (see page 101)

cornflour

royal icing (see page 96)

toothpicks

butterfly mould

baking paper

rolling pin

daisy cutter

tinfoil

Use a toothpick to add colouring paste to the modelling paste and mix in thoroughly – bright colours look great. Lightly dust the butterfly mould with cornflour and press a small amount of paste into the mould. Peel away the mould and lay the butterfly wings on a tray lined with baking paper. Repeat to make as many butterflies as required. Allow to dry overnight.

Dust a work surface with cornflour and roll out some paste to a 2mm thickness. Use the daisy cutter to press out shapes and place on the tray to dry with the butterflies.

To assemble the decorations, mix a little yellow food colouring into the royal icing. Make a paper piping bag (see page 14) and half fill with the royal icing.

Snip the point off the bag so the hole is about 2mm in diameter. Pipe a large dot into the centre of each daisy and leave to dry.

Make a support for the butterflies by bending a doubled sheet of foil into a U shape with a flat bottom. Cut a strip of baking paper 1cm wide to line the base of the U.

Pipe a small dot of icing for the head of the butterfly and join a 1cm long body-shaped line to this. Place a left and right wing into the icing, making sure the wings are V-shaped and inserted well into the icing. Allow to dry overnight.

Peel off the paper and use to decorate your cakes.

Note: Silicon moulds and flower cutters are available from specialty cake-decoration suppliers.

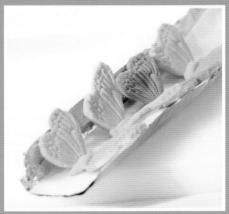

Lace butterflies

royal icing (see page 96)

edible glitter

butterfly template
  (see page 126)

baking paper

tinfoil

Trace the template onto baking paper and place a clean piece of baking paper over the traced design and secure together with tape. Have several pieces of baking paper ready to place over the template as you mass-produce the butterflies with royal icing.

Make a paper piping bag (see page 14) and half fill with white royal icing. Snip the point off the bag so the hole is about 1mm in diameter.

Pipe a thin line of icing over the design, making sure to join the filigree to the sides of the butterfly wings for support. Sprinkle the butterfly wings with edible glitter while wet and allow to dry overnight.

Make a support for the butterflies by bending a doubled sheet of foil into a U shape with a flat bottom. Cut a strip of baking paper 1cm wide to line the base of the U.

Pipe a small dot of icing for the head of the butterfly and join a 1cm long body-shaped line to this. Place a left and right wing into the icing, making sure the wings form a V-shape and are inserted well into the icing. Allow to dry overnight.

Peel off the paper and use to decorate your cakes.

Variation

Use the template on page 122 to make snowflakes.

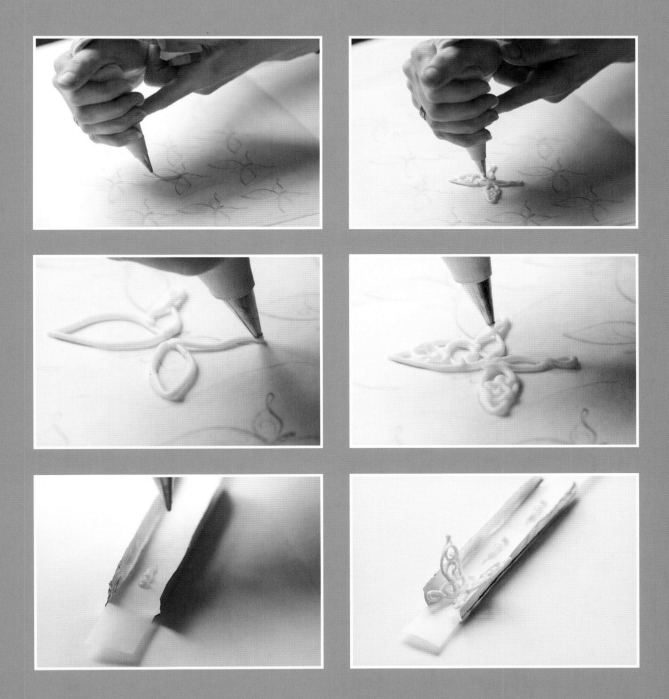

Chocolate filigrees

200g white compound chocolate

200g dark compound chocolate

powder colour for white
   chocolate, if desired

chocolate filigree template
   (see page 128)

baking paper

Trace the template onto baking paper and place a clean piece of baking paper over the traced design and secure together with tape. Have several pieces of baking paper ready to place over the template as you mass-produce the filigree with melted chocolate.

Make two paper piping bags (see page 14).

Melt the white and dark chocolate in separate bowls over a pan of simmering water or in the microwave on low power. Stir until the chocolate is melted and smooth.

Half fill one of the piping bags with white chocolate and fold the top to seal. Snip the point off the piping bag and begin to pipe over the filigree pattern.

Allow to set completely before gently lifting off the paper with a knife.

Meanwhile, repeat with the dark chocolate and use the filigrees to decorate your cakes.

Variation

White chocolate may be coloured, but you will need to use powdered food colouring. Do not use liquid colouring as this will thicken the chocolate and make it hard to pipe. Mix a very small amount of powder into the melted white chocolate and stir until the powder is evenly blended and continue according to the instructions.

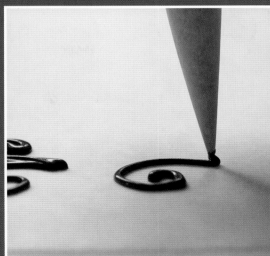

Chocolate spirals

200g chocolate (dark, milk
    or white, as desired)

strips of clean acetate or thick
    plastic about 1cm in width

baking paper

off-set palette knife

1cm wooden dowel or
    wooden spoons

Melt the chocolate over a pan of simmering water or in the microwave on low power. Stir until smooth. Place one of the plastic strips on a piece of baking paper. Spread the strip with melted chocolate.

Leave to sit for 30 seconds before gently picking the strip up and winding it around the dowel or the handle of the wooden spoon. Place the wrapped strip on a piece of baking paper and leave to sit until the chocolate has completely set.

Once set, you will be able to slide the strip off the dowel and peel away the plastic to leave a long chocolate spiral. These are very delicate, so it is advisable to make more than you need to decorate your cakes.

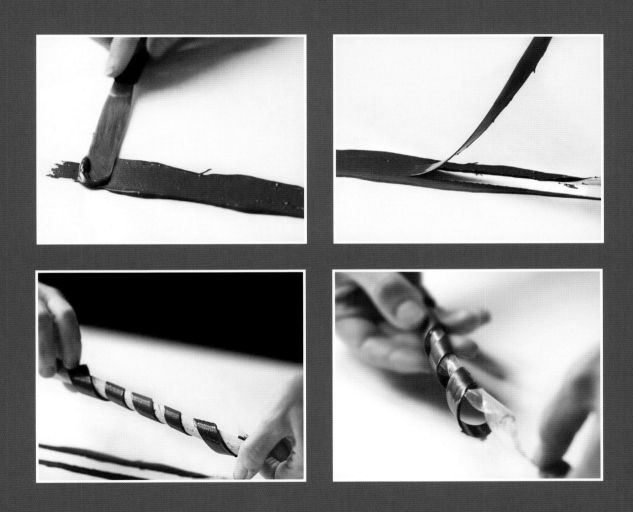

Chocolate cut-outs

250g chocolate (dark, white
   or milk, as desired)

baking paper

tray

off-set palette knife

small cutter

Melt the chocolate over a pan of simmering water or in the microwave on low power. Stir until smooth.

Spread the chocolate over a baking paper-lined tray and leave to semi-set. If the chocolate is too hard it will be brittle and difficult to cut.

Using the cutter, push into the chocolate and remove the cut-out shape. If the chocolate is too soft you can press the cutter into the chocolate then leave the chocolate to finish setting before removing the shape.

The chocolate may also be cut into squares and triangles using a sharp knife. If the chocolate is too hard to cut, the knife can be warmed in boiling water, wiped dry then used to cut the chocolate.

Caramelised cornflakes

350g caster sugar

4 cups cornflakes

Place ½ cup of the sugar into a medium-sized saucepan. Place on the stove over a low heat and allow the sugar to begin to dissolve and melt. Gradually add the remaining sugar, stirring gently to combine after each addition. Be careful not to allow the sugar around the edge of the pan to darken and burn.

Once all the sugar has dissolved and the mix is a golden amber colour, gently stir in the cornflakes. Working quickly, make sure all the cornflakes are sugar coated before tipping the mixture onto a piece of baking paper. Gently pull the cornflakes apart to form small clumps.

Allow to cool until the caramel has set completely before storing in an airtight container for up to 7 days.

Variation

The same method may be used to caramelise whole nuts, such as almonds and hazelnuts. Stir these into the melted sugar and stir to coat with caramel. Tip onto a baking tray and separate the nuts to cool and leave until the caramel has set completely.

Meringues

MAKES ABOUT 30

4 egg whites

pinch of salt

250g caster sugar

2 teaspoons cornflour

1 teaspoon vinegar

Preheat the oven to 150°C. Line two baking trays with baking paper.

Whisk the egg whites and salt with electric beaters until firm peaks are formed, but the eggs whites are not dry. Gradually add the sugar a spoonful at a time, beating well after each addition until the sugar has dissolved. Keep adding the sugar until a glossy mixture is formed and there is no grainy feel to the egg whites. Gently fold in the cornflour and vinegar once the sugar has dissolved. Place the mixture into a piping bag with a 1cm plain nozzle and pipe small circles onto the prepared trays, leaving space between each.

Bake for approximately 35–40 minutes. Turn off the oven and allow the meringues to cool slowly.

Once completely cold, place into an airtight container and store for up to one week.

Gingerbread

115g butter

175g brown sugar

4 tablespoons golden syrup

340g plain flour

1 tablespoon ground ginger

1 teaspoon baking soda

1 egg

Place the butter, sugar and syrup into a saucepan and stir over a low heat until the butter has melted. Sift the flour with the ginger and baking soda into a bowl. Pour in the syrup mixture and the lightly beaten egg. Mix together until a soft dough is formed in the bowl, then tip onto a lightly floured bench and knead into a ball.

Wrap in plastic wrap and refrigerate for 30 minutes.

Preheat the oven to 180°C. Lightly grease a baking tray or line it with baking paper.

Sprinkle some flour onto the work surface and rolling pin. Roll out the dough to 0.5cm thickness. Use your choice of cutters to make shapes and place them on the prepared tray.

Bake for 10 minutes, or until lightly browned.

Allow to cool. Store in an airtight container for up to one week.

Weights & measures

ABBREVIATIONS

g	gram
kg	kilogram
mm	millimetre
cm	centimetre
ml	millilitre
°C	degrees Celsius

CAKE TIN SIZES

Metric	Imperial/US
15cm	6 inches
18cm	7 inches
20cm	8 inches
23cm	9 inches
25cm	10 inches
28cm	11 inches

WEIGHT CONVERSIONS

Metric	Imperial/US
25g	1 oz
50g	2 oz
75g	3 oz
100g	3½ oz
125g	4½ oz
150g	5 oz
175g	6 oz
200g	7 oz
225g	8 oz
250g	9 oz
275g	9½ oz
300g	10½ oz
325g	11½ oz
350g	12½ oz
375g	13 oz
400g	14 oz
450g	16 oz (1 lb)
500g	17½ oz
750g	26½ oz
1kg	35 oz (2¼ lb)

TEMPERATURE CONVERSIONS

Celsius	Fahrenheit	Gas
100°C	225°F	¼
125°C	250°F	½
150°C	300°F	2
160°C	325°F	3
170°C	325°F	3
180°C	350°F	4
190°C	375°F	5
200°C	400°F	6
210°C	425°F	7
220°C	425°F	7
230°C	450°F	8
250°C	500°F	9

LENGTH CONVERSIONS

Metric	Imperial/US
0.5cm (5mm)	¼ inch
1cm	½ inch
2.5cm	1 inch
5cm	2 inches
10cm	4 inches
20cm	8 inches
30cm	12 inches (1 foot)

LIQUID CONVERSIONS

Metric	Imperial	Cup measures
5ml	¼ fl oz	1 teaspoon
15ml	½ fl oz	1 tablespoon
30ml	1 fl oz	⅛ cup
60ml	2 fl oz	¼ cup
125ml	4 fl oz	½ cup
150ml	5 fl oz (¼ pint)	⅔ cup
175ml	6 fl oz	¾ cup
250ml	8 fl oz	1 cup
300ml	10 fl oz (½ pint)	1¼ cups
375ml	12 fl oz	1½ cups
500ml	16 fl oz	2 cups
600ml	20 fl oz (1 pint)	2½ cups

NB The Australian metric tablespoon measures 20ml

Glossary

acetate: clear plastic sheets used in cake decorating. Available from specialty cake-decoration suppliers.

buttermilk: a fermented dairy product with a sour taste. Traditionally the low-fat liquid left after the cream has been removed when making butter. Commercial buttermilk, known as cultured buttermilk, is made from skim milk and milk powder and cultured in the same way as yoghurt.

cachous: tiny edible silver balls used for decorating cakes.

cream of tartar: a by-product of winemaking, cream of tartar has many culinary uses, including stabilising egg whites and preventing sugar syrups from crystallising.

gelatine: this colourless setting agent is available as a powder or in sheets (easier to use) and soaked in cold water before using.

glucose syrup: glucose is a natural form of sugar found in grape juice, honey, corn and certain other vegetables. Glucose syrup is available from pharmacies and some supermarkets.

glycerine: glycerine is a viscous clear oily liquid with a sweet taste. It is manufactured from petroleum or glycerides in fats and, as it is water loving, its culinary uses include preventing ingredients such as dried fruits from getting too dry. Available from pharmacies and some supermarkets.

gum tragacanth: a partially soluble, odourless and tasteless gum used commercially to stabilise, emulsify and thicken foods such as sauces, confectionery and ice cream.

muscovado sugar: dark brown unrefined sugar. Available from most supermarkets.

nonpareilles: small pieces of confectionary used to decorate cakes. Also known as 'sprinkles' or 'hundreds and thousands'.

white vegetable shortening: a semi-solid fat made from hydrogenated vegetable oil, with a higher smoke point and 100% fat content (compared to about 80% for butter and margarine).

Index

Numbers in bold refer to images.

Acknowledgements

I would like to take this opportunity to thank those who have helped me create and indulge my passion for cupcakes. A big heartfelt thank you to:

Our panel of tasters who had the unenviable job of trying the recipes and helping me decide which cakes were the best for the book.

The Tempt team, especially Rebecca, Maria, Ellie and Danielle, who have all helped to bring the Tempt store to life. Their enthusiasm has been an inspiration.

My mum, dad and sister who have come along for the ride and who always knew I could do it, even when I didn't.

The team at New Holland Publishers, especially Louise for her patience with a new and naïve writer.

The amazing photographers, Danielle and Adam, who did such a brilliant job of photographing the cakes and capturing the mood I had in mind.

To our children Maddie, Dani and Max who sit in the kitchen patiently while I bake and never complain when there isn't a spare cake for them, but always tell me when the cupcakes look great. (Sometimes they get to lick the bowl!)

To my partner Adam whose patience and support is unfailing, as is his belief in me.

Thanks to you all.

Tamara Jane

Templates

Use any of the following templates (or make up your own) by tracing multiple times onto baking paper. Place another sheet of baking paper on top and, using a paper piping bag filled with royal icing or chocolate, pipe a thin line of icing over the design. Allow to dry overnight before carefully removing from the paper and using to decorate your cakes.

Lace Butterflies

Lace Snowflakes

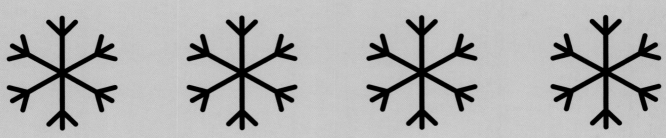

Filigree 1

Filigree 2

Filigree 3